AMERICAN DESERTS

WILLIAM K SMITHEY

GALLERY BOOKS
An Imprint of W. H. Smith Publishers Inc.
112 Madison Avenue
New York City 10016

Text
William K. Smithey

Design
Clive Dorman

Jacket Design
Claire Leighton

Commissioning Editor
Andrew Preston

Publishing Assistant
Edward Doling

Editorial
Gill Waugh

Production
Ruth Arthur
David Proffit
Sally Connolly
Andrew Whitelaw

Director of Production
Gerald Hughes

Director of Publishing
David Gibbon

Photography
Planet Earth Pictures:
Ron W. Bohr 18, 28 *top*; Franz J. Camenzind 15 *bottom*, 17 *top*;
D. Robert Franz 13 *center*, 17 *bottom*; Robert A. Juriet 7 *top*, 26-27, 27
top, 28 *bottom*, 31 *bottom*; A. Kerstitch 8 *top*, 9 *top*, 10 *bottom*; Ken King 8
center; Ken Lucas 8 *bottom*, 9 *bottom*, 12, 16 *bottom*, 19; Dave Lyons 4, 6,
22-23, 24; John & Gillian Lythgoe 20; John Lythgoe 5, 10 *top*, 11, 29, 31
top, front and back covers; David E. Rowley 7 *bottom*, 13 *bottom*, 15 *top*;
William K. Smithey 14, 21, 25, 30-31 *bottom*, 32; Joyce Wilson 13 *top*.

CLB 2486
This edition published in 1990 by Gallery Books,
an imprint of WH Smith Publishers, Inc,
112 Madison Avenue, New York 10016.
© 1990 Colour Library Books Ltd, Godalming, Surrey, England.
All rights reserved.
Colour separations by Scantrans Pte Ltd, Singapore.
Printed and bound by New Interlitho, Italy.
ISBN 0 8317 6978 5

Gallery Books are available for bulk purchase for sales promotions
and premium use. For details write or telephone
the Manager of Special Sales, WH Smith Publishers, Inc,
112 Madison Avenue, New York, New York 10016 (212) 532-6600.

CONTENTS

INTRODUCTION

Many people think of the desert as simply a dry place, a sandy wasteland of occasional low cacti where few things survive and it is always hot. This is a misconception. While the one common factor defining a desert is dryness, the deserts of the United States are anything but sandy wastelands. Instead they are places full of life well adapted to this harsh environment. A desert is a place where heat, cold and scarcity of water conspire against life and where life, with its talent for survival, responds in a multitude of ways.

While most American deserts receive an average of less than ten inches of rainfall each year, not everywhere with this little rainfall is a desert. Since it is the low availability of water to plants and animals that defines a desert, a second ingredient, a high potential for evaporation, is also important. High winds, ample sunshine and intense heat, all characteristic of American deserts, contribute to evaporating the scarce moisture. In some areas the potential for evaporation is many times greater than the rainfall.

The enormous difference between rates of rainfall and evaporation contributes much to the dryness of deserts, but the pattern of rainfall throughout the year is also important. Deserts typically have highly variable rainfall that occurs infrequently and as distinct events. Intense summer thundershowers may be very short in duration and quickly yield to the drying summer sun. Winter precipitation falls when many plants are dormant, and may fall as snow.

Clouds act as insulators, retaining some of the heat acquired at the earth's surface during the day. Lacking the insulating effect of clouds, deserts cannot retain their heat, and therefore suffer wide extremes of temperature every twenty-four hours. These conditions pose additional problems for desert dwellers.

Despite all these adverse conditions, many plants and animals have successfully adapted to the desert regime. The scarcity of water is overcome by various adaptations. For example, many predators obtain sufficient moisture to survive from their prey, while other animals have evolved to use whatever water is available efficiently. Plants cope partly by growing during the more favorable parts of the year. Some plants have seeds that will only grow when water is available, while others store water in their trunks when it is plentiful for use when it is scarce.

Below: a forest of saguaro and jumping cactus in the subtropical Sonoran Desert's Ajo Mountains. Facing page: barrel cactus, brittlebush and agave on the low hills of the Anza Borrego Desert, California.

LOCATION

Much of the North American desert is located between the Rocky Mountains in the east and the Sierra Nevada in the west. Within these nearly 500,000 square miles lie four distinct desert areas. The largest of these and the furthest north, the Great Basin Desert, is a cold desert, a place where over half the precipitation falls as snow. It occupies the southern third of Idaho, the southeastern corner of Oregon, the western half of Utah and most of Nevada. The three hot desert areas, where precipitation usually falls as rain, lie to the south of the Great Basin and include the Sonoran Desert in Arizona and California, the Mojave Desert of southern Nevada and part of California and the Chihuahuan Desert, which lies mostly in Mexico but extends into southern New Mexico and the extreme west of Texas.

These are all dry places but, in part because of the large geographical areas involved, the climate within these four deserts varies greatly. In the south, the lush, subtropical Sonoran Desert has two reliable rainy seasons and moderate winter temperatures. The Chihuahuan Desert, which extends up from Mexico in four finger-like projections, has fairly generous rainfall and, because it is an area of high elevations, is known for its low winter temperatures. The Death Valley portion of the Mojave Desert may go a year without measurable rain and is the hottest place in North America.

Facing page: (top) snow-covered sand dunes in White Sands National Monument, New Mexico, and (bottom) Great Sand Dunes National Monument, Colorado. Above: Delicate Arch, Arches National Park, Utah, and (below) salt flats on the floor of Death Valley, California.

INTRODUCTION TO DESERT ANIMALS

All animals need water, a scarce commodity in the desert. Animals also suffer in extremes of cold or heat, and parts of the American desert can be bitterly cold in the winter and oppressively hot in the summer. This combination of drought and temperature extremes affects animal life in a number of different ways.

REPTILES

Reptiles are often called "cold-blooded," but this is a misnomer. Reptiles are ectotherms, animals that gain their body heat from an external source, the sun. By following a daily routine, they maintain their body temperature at the most efficient level. This is in contrast to mammals and birds, which as endotherms maintain their body temperatures using internal mechanisms. While endothermy has advantages, they come at a high energy cost. A reptile can survive on ten percent of the nourishment that a mammal of similar size would require.

Because they are so energy efficient, reptiles are especially well suited to desert environments. In addition, their tough skins retard moisture loss and most can survive on the moisture of prey animals. They are fairly tolerant of heat, but they do have their limits. Most snakes will die if exposed for prolonged periods to temperatures of over 100° F. Lizards, which unlike snakes have legs and therefore carry their bodies away from the searing heat right at the surface, can survive somewhat higher temperatures.

Lizards are the most conspicuous animals in the desert. They vary in size from the three- or four-inch-long yucca night lizard to the two-foot-long Gila monster. Most are insect eaters but two, the chuckwalla and the desert crested lizard, are strict vegetarians. Many scurry around, running over rocks and up the trunks of desert trees looking for insects. Others, especially horned lizards, blend into the desert soil and wait for a passing beetle or ant. Some are legless, but most have four legs.

Lizards have evolved many defense

Top: a collared lizard raising its temperature by basking on a boulder and (center) the chuckwalla, a herbivore that eats buds, flowers and fruits. Since it feeds mainly on ants, the ominous appearance of a horned lizard (right) is purely defensive, being designed to scare away predators.

mechanisms to discourage other animals from eating them. The chuckwalla lives among boulders and when alarmed it wedges itself between them and inflates. It becomes so thoroughly jammed that it cannot be removed. If threatened, horned lizards will spray blood from a pore in the lower eyelid. They can shoot from both eyes at once and hit a target as far away as four feet.

Snakes are much less common in desert areas than lizards. While a few small snakes eat insects and other invertebrates, most feed on other vertebrates – lizards, other snakes, rodents and even rabbits. Most are harmless to man, but the bites of rattlesnakes and the Arizona coral snake can be deadly.

The rosy boa, found in the Sonoran and Mojave deserts, is a powerful constrictor that hunts small mammals and birds. Perhaps the fastest snake is the coachwhip, which uses its speed during daylight hunting of grasshoppers, cicadas, lizards, snakes and small rodents. The western blind snake eats ants and termites, which it locates by following the odors left by their trails.

The swift coachwhip (above) is found on rocky hillsides and in desert scrub. Below: the rosy boa, a nocturnal hunter that is primarily terrestrial but will occasionally climb shrubs in search of prey.

POISONOUS REPTILES

Rattlesnakes, which are only found in the Americas, are predators and feed on mice, rabbits, ground squirrels and occasional ground-nesting birds, insects and lizards. There are over thirty species and all have rattles.

Rattlesnakes inject venom using hypodermic-like fangs. The front fangs, which retract and lie flat against the gums when the mouth is closed, raise and point forward to inject poison when the animal strikes. The toxin subdues prey and also contains enzymes that, once injected, begin to break down the prey for digestion. Since snakes swallow their prey whole, this softening action makes a meal easier to ingest.

The "rattle" is a noise producing device made up of a series of loosely attached horny rings at the extreme tip of the tail. When vibrated it produces a hissing or buzzing sound. The rattle increases in length with each molt but, since the oldest rattles on the very tip of the tail wear out, the number of rattles is not a clear indication of a snake's age. The purpose of the rattle is not fully understood, but it is believed to be defensive, used as a threat during potentially harmful situations.

Of the thousands of lizard species throughout the world, only two are venomous. One of these is the Gila monster of the Sonoran desert, which is also one of the world's largest lizards. Unlike

rattlesnakes, which inject their venom, the Gila monster lets the poison flow into the victim as it chews on it. Its bite is rarely fatal to humans, and its staple food consists of the eggs of reptiles and birds.

The upper fangs of a rattlesnake (above) are used to inject venom into prey or for defense. When confronted, rattlesnakes assume a defensive posture (facing page), rattling their tails. The poisonous Gila monster (below) is nocturnal and its bite is rarely fatal to humans.

DESERT TORTOISE

The desert tortoise lives in the deserts of the southwestern United States and northwestern Mexico. Once widespread and occurring in far greater numbers, it is now an animal very much threatened by man's activities.

Much of the life of a tortoise, up to nine months each year, is spent underground. It hibernates from September or October and emerges in late February to early April. Tortoises leave their burrows in the spring, when they feed on a wide range of flowers and grasses. They retreat to their burrows again with the onset of high summer temperatures for a period of inactivity called estivation. During droughts they spend additional time underground, surviving on water and fat stored in their bodies during more plentiful times.

Tortoises may live to be between sixty and eighty or more years of age and require a long period to reach reproductive maturity. Once sexually mature, the females dig a nest and lay from four to twelve table-tennis-ball-sized eggs. As the two-inch-long hatchlings emerge from their underground nest they must immediately find shelter from the climate and predators. With a shell as thin as a human fingernail, they are tender morsels and as few as four of every hundred hatchlings will live to maturity. Not until they are four to five inches long and seven years of age will a bony skeleton have developed under the shell.

MAMMALS

Desert mammals are abundant but, because many are nocturnal, they are seldom seen by the casual observer. Most desert mammals are rodents that feed on the enormous supply of plant seeds. Far less numerous are mammals that eat foliage. These browsers include bighorn sheep, rabbits and antelopes. Next in abundance are the carnivores, such as coyotes, bobcats and mountain lions, and least abundant are the insect-eating mammals, such as bats and shrews.

Mammals have adapted to desert life in various ways. Some large mammals migrate to other areas during the worst of the year, while those who stay spend the heat of the day bedded down in the shade. Small mammals lie in underground burrows or the deep shade beneath boulders. Some desert mammals have diminished their requirements for liquid and can extract enough to live from their

The desert tortoise (below) is adapted to its subterranean life, having heavily scaled front legs which are perfect for digging. The thick shell of a mature tortoise provides effective protection from predators. The most widely distributed cat in America, the mountain lion or cougar (facing page top and facing page center) is a strongly territorial and solitary hunter that is found in mountainous desert areas throughout the western United States. The black-tailed jack rabbit (facing page bottom) is widespread throughout the West. Its enormous ears help to dissipate excessive heat.

food. These animals may never drink at all.

In spite of a diet dominated by dry seeds, the kangaroo rat has reduced its need for water to the point where it can survive on very little. To drastically minimize their water loss, they don't sweat or pant and stay cool by avoiding heat. In addition, their kidneys concentrate waste up to five times more than those of man and the droppings of the kangaroo rat contain very little moisture. All animals produce a small amount of water within their own body as food is digested. Kangaroo rats are so efficient in their water use that this metabolic water, though small in amount, is sufficient for its needs.

OTHER SMALL MAMMALS

Some small mammals can be found in parts of all four American deserts. They include Merriam's kangaroo rat, the Yuma myotis bat, the white-tailed antelope squirrel, the black-tailed jack rabbit and both kit and gray foxes. Others are more geographically limited. The coati and collared peccary are found only in the Sonoran and Chihuahuan deserts, as is the antelope jack rabbit. The Great Basin pocket mouse and chisel-toothed kangaroo rat are distributed widely throughout the Great Basin, while the pale kangaroo mouse is limited to central Nevada.

DESERT BIGHORN SHEEP

Wild sheep, along with their kin the buffaloes, cattle, goats and antelopes, are widespread throughout the world. The desert bighorn sheep is found throughout the warmer desert regions of southwestern North America. It requires steep, rugged terrain with adequate food, access to water and freedom from undue competition from other mammals, including man.

The most conspicuous features of male bighorns are their massive, permanent horns. During the mating season the male sheep use these impressive horns in spectacular battles for the right to mate with females. This fighting consists primarily of head butting and tests both the stamina and skill of the rams. In part because a mature ram's skull may be one inch or more in thickness, this dramatic head butting results in few serious injuries.

Bighorn populations have been much reduced in recent years. Coyote and mountain lions are the biggest predators of adult bighorns, while the young are prey to such animals as gray foxes, bobcats and golden eagles. However, natural predators are not the important factor in the decline of bighorns. Rather it is the loss of habitat to man and the introduction of diseases from domestic animals, mostly sheep and cattle, that have had such an impact on the sheep population.

Male desert bighorn sheep (below) are agile climbers inhabiting areas rarely visited by man.

WILD HORSES AND FERAL BURROS

Neither feral burros nor wild horses are naturally found in North America. Introduced by early explorers and miners, they faced few natural predators and, as a result, their populations increased dramatically. Wild horses can be found today in ten western states, with most living in the Great Basin. Burros, once the trusty companions of early prospectors, have escaped or were released in sufficient numbers to become successful wild residents of the desert. Together, burros and wild horses compete with both domestic animals and native species for both water and forage and are controversial members of the desert fauna.

Although their ancestors were native to America, today's wild horses (this page) are introduced. They have few natural predators and have thrived in desert regions.

DESERT BIRDS

Birds are abundant in arid lands, but they show little of the specialization in appearance or form exhibited by other desert animals. Shade is absolutely essential to all desert birds, and there are many examples of birds that shelter in nests, rock overhangs, trees and dense shrubs. While a few, like the burrowing owl, use abandoned mammal burrows, the large majority must cope with conditions above ground. Birds are the most mobile of animals and many simply leave the desert when it is too cold, dry or hot.

One bird that does not leave is the sage grouse. This is a fowl-sized bird with a gray-brown colored pattern that blends well with the sagebrush of the arid plains where it is found. Sage grouse live almost exclusively on sagebrush leaves during autumn and winter, when there is very little else to eat.

The mating ritual of the sage grouse involves elaborate, competitive displays on a traditional site known as a lek. On these leks, used by generations of sage grouse, the males hold individual territories, the central territories being the most

prized. The dominant male usually claims the central position, with a hierarchy of lesser males around him. A male's success in attracting and mating with females correlates with its position on the lek. As a result, relatively few males sire most of the young.

The *Phainopepla* is a black bird with a prominent crest and white wing patches that are revealed as it flies. *Phainopepla*, derived from the Greek meaning shining robe, is both its common and scientific name. Widespread in the deserts of the Southwest, it is usually found along dry washes where underground water courses provide enough water for mesquite to grow. The *Phainopepla* eats the berries of mistletoe, which grows as a parasite in mesquite, and hunts flying insects.

The road runner, a member of the cuckoo family, is a comical resident of the southern deserts. It spends most of its time on the ground, can run as fast as fifteen miles per hour and preys mostly on lizards, snakes, rodents and birds.

Road runners nest in cacti or other thorny bushes and they provide water for their young in a unique way. A parent will arrive at the nest with prey in its beak and thrust it into the nestling's beak without releasing it. While the two remain locked together, liquid that is produced in the parent's stomach as part of the digestive process trickles down into the youngster's mouth.

Gambel's quails are found throughout the arid southwest of the United States and northwest Mexico. They are most abundant in the Sonoran Desert of southern Arizona, where they are found in mesquite thickets or among willows growing in low river valleys. Their principal food is mesquite beans and the fruits of several cacti.

Woodpeckers feed on adult insects and larvae found in the bark of trees. The ladder-backed woodpecker is a desert resident that, in addition to feeding like other woodpeckers, has a mutually advantageous relationship with the century plant. The century plant is pollinated by the agave beetle, which also lays eggs in its flower stalk. The larvae, which if left unchecked would eat all the seeds, are food for the ladder-backed woodpecker. When the century plant seeds mature the plant dies and the woodpecker uses the flower stalk as a nest site.

Top: two male sage grouse, with tail feathers erect, court a female on a display ground or lek. Far left: a road runner, a masterful hunter, capturing a lizard and (left) young burrowing owls outside their den.

DESERT INSECTS SPIDERS AND SCORPIONS

The large majority of desert invertebrates – animals lacking back bones – are insects and their relatives the spiders and scorpions. Crickets and grasshoppers are particularly well adapted to the desert and are often seen foraging during the day. Wasps, flies and beetles become abundant when flowers are in bloom. Bees are common throughout the year. Insects, in turn, provide much of the food for small desert mammals.

With its hairy legs and relatively large size, the desert tarantula can look threatening to man. It is not. The desert tarantula is only harmful to the insects, lizards and other small animals upon which it feeds. As formidable as the tarantula is, it too has enemies. The tarantula hawk wasp uses the spider to feed its young. It paralyzes the tarantula with its sting, then drags it to an underground den where it lays an egg on the still-living spider. After hatching, the larval wasp feeds on the spider without immediately killing it. The spider eventually dies, but not until the young wasp has fed enough to mature.

Unlike the tarantula, desert scorpions inflict a painful sting which can, in some cases, be dangerous to man. Scorpions attack their prey using a large stinger and a poison gland at the base of the tail. They may also use their stinger defensively against man and, while most stings are not of any consequence, they can be quite painful. One potentially dangerous type, the *Centruroides* scorpion, lives in the Sonoran Desert of Arizona. Stings from these creatures require immediate medical attention and can be fatal.

Below: a desert tarantula, impressive but harmless.
Facing page top: a Centruroides *scorpion. Its prey is captured with its forelegs and killed with its tail's sting.*
Facing page bottom: a female scorpion carrying her young.

DESERT PLANTS

Plants put down roots. They can't occupy burrows or migrate to a cooler spot for the summer, nor can they move in search of water. Because they lack mobility they have evolved the ability to tolerate drought or to avoid it. Cacti have fleshy stems which store water in times of plenty and leaves reduced to spines to minimise water loss. The seeds of many desert plants will not sprout until sufficient rain has fallen to maximise their chances of survival. Once conditions are right, they grow quickly, flower and make new seeds. The common creosote bush has an exceptionally shallow and extensive root system that allows it to use the thin film of water formed by the dew at the surface of the soil.

Heat and cold are also problems for plants. Many plants simply go dormant during the coldest parts of the year. Plants rely on the sun for energy, but the extreme heat of some deserts poses a special set of problems. Desert holly, a common desert shrub, grows with leaves oriented so that during much of the day the sun falls only on their edges. Only in the mornings, when the sun is low and less intense, are the leaves exposed to direct sunlight.

The creosote bush (facing page top) is characteristic of North America's hot deserts, often growing in groups that are clones. Facing page bottom: the sandy desert in bloom, and (below) the showy yellow flowers of barrel cactus, which grow in a circular crown.

SPRING WILDFLOWERS

As the cool of winter yields to the warmth of spring, desert plants put on a show. When all the conditions are just right, with rains spread evenly through the winter and the spring warm but not too hot, the desert will burst into flower. The apparently barren earth is covered by a lush carpet of wildflowers and the green stems of cactus, swollen with stored water, sprout vivid blooms. Desert bushes and trees that, at first glance, appear to be nothing but a formidable thicket of spines, put forth delicate blossoms.

For annuals – plants that grow, flower and set seed in a single season – the trick is to flower only when conditions are adequate for success. Some desert annuals have seeds that will not germinate unless they are thoroughly soaked. Another characteristic of many annuals is that, during a dry season, they can form stunted plants with a few flowers. Thus they can ripen a few seeds in even the most difficult conditions.

Perennials, plants that live from year to year, respond with a different set of strategies. Some, such as the Ocotillo, remain dormant until adequate rain falls. When sufficient moisture is present, Ocotillo quickly put out leaves and brilliant red flowers. Cacti, which store water in their stems to counteract the worst of a drought, sprout flowers among their spines. Because competition for pollinators is fierce during the short spring, some perennials, such as the smoke tree, postpone flowering until later in the summer.

SAND DUNES

While the common image of deserts includes miles upon miles of sand dunes, in fact they make up but a small percentage of the American deserts. At first glance, sand dunes look as sterile as any place in the desert environment. They are not; however, shifting sand is a particularly difficult place to make a home.

One animal obviously adapted to the shifting sands is the fringe-toed lizard, which gets its name from the comblike fringe of pointed scales on the trailing edge of its toes. These toe fringes help to stop its feet from sinking as it scampers over the sand looking for insects to eat. When frightened, or to avoid extremes of heat or cold, the fringe-toed lizard "dives" into the sand. To keep the sand out when burrowing it has a set-back jaw, scaly flaps over each ear, overlapping eyelids, and valves in its nostrils.

Insects too make the dunes their home. The sand roach spends virtually all its time below the surface, swimming through loose sand. While the adult males have wings, the pre-adults and adult females do not, spending all their time in the dunes. Males emerge to fly only at night.

Moving on sand is a challenge for all animals, but it is especially hard for snakes. On firm surfaces, a snake normally moves forward by flexing the muscles of its body against the ground. But on loose sand this method results in the sand moving rather than the snake. The sidewinder rattlesnake has evolved a unique method of moving over sand dunes. It throws a loop of its body sideways, thus creating enough momentum for the rest of its body to be able to follow. The repetition of this action results in a series of parallel tracks quite unlike the linear pattern typical of other snakes.

During the summer the surface temperature of the tall sand dunes of Great Sand Dunes National Monument, Colorado, can reach 140° F.

WHEN WATER ACCUMULATES

DESERT FISH

While most people do not associate fishes with deserts, arid areas do contain widely spaced springs and small streams which are often inhabited by tiny fish. As the southwest dried out over the last 2,000 to 20,000 years, these fish have persisted in scattered permanent water sites that are the remnants of much more extensive bodies of water.

One of the most interesting of these small fish is the minnow-sized pupfish. In the Death Valley area, the hottest and driest part of the United States, there are twenty isolated pupfish sites with ten distinct types of fish. During the breeding season, males vigorously defend territories. The breeding season typically extends over seven or eight months and in some warm springs some individuals may breed year round.

Fresno Spring (facing page) in Big Bend National Park, Texas, provides an oasis of fresh water. Below: spawning Salt Creek pupfish. The larger male displays breeding colors. This pupfish lives only in Salt Creek, a saline stream flowing on the floor of Death Valley, California.

LIFE IN A TEMPORARY POOL

In contrast to life in a permanent stream or lake, animals living in temporary pools must respond quickly to the presence of standing water.

The Great Basin spadefoot toad is well adapted to life in temporary pools. It spends up to nine months, during the hottest, driest part of the year, under the surface of the ground. Aided by a horny projection on its rear feet, it burrows up to three feet under the surface in search of a moist habitat. When the conditions are right, it develops an outer coat to its skin that will harden and form a watertight seal except for two holes at the nostrils.

When there is sufficient rain the toad emerges and races to complete its life cycle. As temporary pools form the toads mate and clusters of eggs are laid. Immediately, the adults begin to feed in preparation for returning below ground. From the eggs hatch tadpoles which mature into toads in as little as four to six weeks – much less time than the two months of the typical non-desert toad.

Another resident of temporary puddles is a tiny crustacean called the fairy shrimp. Fairy shrimp develop from eggs that may have been blowing in the desert dust for many years. These tiny crustaceans also compress their life cycle into the short period for which the puddle exists.

Desert Lakes

All of the permanent lakes found in the American deserts have no outlets to the sea. The largest of these lakes is the Great Salt Lake in Utah. Others include Pyramid (which is just barely salty), Owens (now dry) and Mono lakes. The rivers and streams that flow into these lakes carry minute concentrations of minerals which eventually concentrate to levels that become toxic to many plants and animals. Animals that live in these mineral rich lakes have developed unique adaptations to these harsh environments.

Mono Lake, located just east of Yosemite National Park, is fed by water rushing down the eastern escarpment of the Sierra Nevada Mountains. In the 700,000 years since it formed, Mono Lake has concentrated minerals until today its water is three times as salty and eighty times as alkaline as the ocean. Few species inhabit the lake but those that do often exist in huge numbers. With no fish as predators, uncounted millions of brine shrimp flourish by devouring algae. Brine flies darken miles of lake shoreline.

The brine flies and shrimp together provide easy meals for the seventy-nine species of water bird that visit Mono's shores. For five species in particular the lake serves a critical need. California

gulls and snowy plovers nest around the lake, while Wilson's phalaropes, red-necked phalaropes and eared grebes use the lake during migration.

Also a result of its chemistry are the strange mineral formations, called tufa, along its shores. While tufa is present in other alkaline lakes, only at Mono does it grow into various towers, knobs and mushrooming spires. Tufa is formed in the lake where freshwater springs bubble up through its sandy bottom. The calcium in spring water combines with the alkaline lake water to form tufa.

Right: brine flies flourish along Mono Lake's shoreline and (below) tufa towers rise above its surface.

SAGUARO CACTUS WILDLIFE

Of all the American deserts, the Sonoran has the most generous rain schedule. Here, instead of the typical single period of precipitation, there are two reliable rainy seasons. Winter brings long duration, low intensity rains; summer shorter, more intense precipitation. The result is a desert with tall forests of saguaro cactus, a sharp contrast to the seemingly endless miles of sagebrush that characterize the Great Basin or the acres of low creosote of the Chihuahuan and the Mojave deserts. It is, perhaps, the American desert as it is most often pictured.

The slow-growing saguaro cactus can reach a height of fifty feet and is a focus of wildlife activity. Its flowers, which bloom at night, are pollinated by two different nectar-feeding bats and the resulting fruits are eaten by both rodents and bats. Birds such as the Gila woodpecker and gilded flicker hollow nests along the trunk. When these nests are abandoned a new wave of residents, including western screech-owls, elf owls, flycatchers and purple martins, move in. Still later rats, mice and lizards may occupy the well-used holes.

Wildlife activity is not limited to the trunk. Red-tailed hawks build large stick nests at the base of the saguaro's branches and white-winged doves nest further along them. Spiders, insects and even lizards live within the pleats along the trunk. These interrelationships between plant and animal species are an example of the vital links among all living things, in the desert as well as elsewhere.

Saguaro flowers (above) open only at night. The fruits are edible. Below: a barrel cactus in bloom. These plants, which may grow to ten feet in height, are also known as fishhook cacti because of their inward curling spines. Facing page: a red-tailed hawk uses the top of a saguaro cactus as a perch while feeding.

DESERT CONSERVATION

The North American deserts, which once seemed so vast, are becoming increasingly fragmented. The desert environment is a fragile one and the plants and animals within it are suffering from the increasing presence of man. The lack of water in the desert has limited man's impact there, but, having considerable mineral wealth, dependably clear weather and reservoirs of alternative energy, the American deserts are under increasing pressure. Additionally, they serve as an unfenced recreation area – a playground for a burgeoning human population eager to escape the congestion and polluted air of large cities.

Wildlife has suffered with the more frequent presence of man. Desert bighorn sheep numbers have declined due to exposure to and competition with domestic livestock. Desert tortoise numbers have decreased because of habitat destruction, competition with livestock and road casualties, and the lowering of water tables by the mining of

groundwater has devastated some pupfish populations. The welfare of these and other desert creatures depends on our understanding of the fragile nature of their environment and our willingness to ensure that it is preserved.

Left: mesas rise above Monument Valley Tribal Park, Arizona. Below left: native palm trees at sunrise in Seventeen Palms Oasis, Anza Borrego Desert State Park, California. Below: desert scrub growing on a dormant volcano near Mono Lake, and (overleaf) Joshua Tree National Monument, both in the California.